Scarsdale
Diet Journal

Yap Kee Chong
8345 NW 66 ST #B7885
Miami, FL 33166

Createspace

THIS JOURNAL BELONGS TO

Scarsdale Diet

DATE: / /

DAILY INTAKE

BREAKFAST

CALORIES

SNACK

CALORIES

LUNCH

CALORIES

SNACK

CALORIES

DINNER

CALORIES

WORKOUT

NOTES

Scarsdale Diet

DATE: / /

DAILY INTAKE

BREAKFAST

CALORIES

SNACK

CALORIES

LUNCH

CALORIES

SNACK

CALORIES

DINNER

CALORIES

WORKOUT

NOTES

Scarsdale Diet

DAILY INTAKE

BREAKFAST

CALORIES

SNACK

CALORIES

LUNCH

CALORIES

SNACK

CALORIES

DINNER

CALORIES

WORKOUT

NOTES

Scarsdale Diet

DATE: / /

DAILY INTAKE

BREAKFAST

CALORIES

SNACK

CALORIES

LUNCH

CALORIES

SNACK

CALORIES

DINNER

CALORIES

WORKOUT

NOTES

Scarsdale Diet

DATE: / /

DAILY INTAKE

BREAKFAST

CALORIES

SNACK

CALORIES

LUNCH

CALORIES

WORKOUT

SNACK

CALORIES

NOTES

DINNER

CALORIES

Scarsdale Diet

DATE: ___ / ___ / ___

DAILY INTAKE

BREAKFAST

CALORIES

SNACK

CALORIES

LUNCH

CALORIES

SNACK

CALORIES

DINNER

CALORIES

WORKOUT

NOTES

Scarsdale Diet

DATE: /   /

DAILY INTAKE

BREAKFAST

CALORIES

SNACK

CALORIES

LUNCH

CALORIES

SNACK

CALORIES

DINNER

CALORIES

WORKOUT

NOTES

Scarsdale Diet

DATE: / /

DAILY INTAKE

BREAKFAST

CALORIES

SNACK

CALORIES

LUNCH

CALORIES

SNACK

CALORIES

WORKOUT

DINNER

CALORIES

NOTES

Scarsdale Diet

DATE: / /

DAILY INTAKE

BREAKFAST

CALORIES

SNACK

CALORIES

LUNCH

CALORIES

SNACK

CALORIES

DINNER

CALORIES

WORKOUT

NOTES

Scarsdale Diet

DATE: / /

DAILY INTAKE

BREAKFAST

CALORIES

SNACK

CALORIES

LUNCH

CALORIES

SNACK

CALORIES

DINNER

CALORIES

WORKOUT

NOTES

Scarsdale Diet

DATE: / /

DAILY INTAKE

BREAKFAST

CALORIES

SNACK

CALORIES

LUNCH

CALORIES

SNACK

CALORIES

DINNER

CALORIES

WORKOUT

NOTES

Scarsdale Diet

DATE: / /

DAILY INTAKE

BREAKFAST

CALORIES

SNACK

CALORIES

LUNCH

CALORIES

SNACK

CALORIES

DINNER

CALORIES

WORKOUT

NOTES

Scarsdale Diet

DATE: / /

DAILY INTAKE

BREAKFAST

CALORIES

SNACK

CALORIES

LUNCH

CALORIES

SNACK

CALORIES

DINNER

CALORIES

WORKOUT

NOTES

Scarsdale Diet

DATE: /   /

DAILY INTAKE

BREAKFAST

CALORIES

SNACK

CALORIES

LUNCH

CALORIES

SNACK

CALORIES

DINNER

CALORIES

WORKOUT

NOTES

Scarsdale Diet

DATE: / /

DAILY INTAKE

BREAKFAST

CALORIES

SNACK

CALORIES

LUNCH

CALORIES

SNACK

CALORIES

DINNER

CALORIES

WORKOUT

NOTES

Scarsdale Diet

DATE: / /

DAILY INTAKE

BREAKFAST

CALORIES

SNACK

CALORIES

LUNCH

CALORIES

SNACK

CALORIES

DINNER

CALORIES

WORKOUT

NOTES

Scarsdale Diet

DAILY INTAKE

BREAKFAST

CALORIES

SNACK

CALORIES

LUNCH

CALORIES

SNACK

CALORIES

DINNER

CALORIES

WORKOUT

NOTES

Scarsdale Diet

DATE: / /

DAILY INTAKE

BREAKFAST

CALORIES

SNACK

CALORIES

LUNCH

CALORIES

SNACK

CALORIES

DINNER

CALORIES

WORKOUT

NOTES

Scarsdale Diet

DAILY INTAKE

BREAKFAST

CALORIES

SNACK

CALORIES

LUNCH

CALORIES

SNACK

CALORIES

DINNER

CALORIES

WORKOUT

NOTES

Scarsdale Diet

DATE: / /

DAILY INTAKE

BREAKFAST

CALORIES

SNACK

CALORIES

LUNCH

CALORIES

SNACK

CALORIES

DINNER

CALORIES

WORKOUT

NOTES

Scarsdale Diet

DATE: __ / __ / __

DAILY INTAKE

BREAKFAST

CALORIES

SNACK

CALORIES

LUNCH

CALORIES

SNACK

CALORIES

DINNER

CALORIES

WORKOUT

NOTES

Scarsdale Diet

DAILY INTAKE

BREAKFAST

CALORIES

SNACK

CALORIES

LUNCH

CALORIES

SNACK

CALORIES

DINNER

CALORIES

WORKOUT

NOTES

Scarsdale Diet

DATE: / /

DAILY INTAKE

BREAKFAST

CALORIES

SNACK

CALORIES

LUNCH

CALORIES

SNACK

CALORIES

DINNER

CALORIES

WORKOUT

NOTES

Scarsdale Diet

DATE: / /

DAILY INTAKE

BREAKFAST

CALORIES

SNACK

CALORIES

LUNCH

CALORIES

SNACK

CALORIES

DINNER

CALORIES

WORKOUT

NOTES

Scarsdale Diet

DATE: / /

DAILY INTAKE

BREAKFAST

CALORIES

SNACK

CALORIES

LUNCH

CALORIES

SNACK

CALORIES

DINNER

CALORIES

WORKOUT

NOTES

Scarsdale Diet

DAILY INTAKE

BREAKFAST

CALORIES

SNACK

CALORIES

LUNCH

CALORIES

SNACK

CALORIES

DINNER

CALORIES

WORKOUT

NOTES

Scarsdale Diet

DATE: ___ / ___ / ___

DAILY INTAKE

BREAKFAST

CALORIES

SNACK

CALORIES

LUNCH

CALORIES

SNACK

CALORIES

DINNER

CALORIES

WORKOUT

NOTES

Scarsdale Diet

DATE: _____ / _____ / _____

DAILY INTAKE

BREAKFAST | CALORIES

SNACK | CALORIES

LUNCH | CALORIES

SNACK | CALORIES

DINNER | CALORIES

WORKOUT

NOTES

Scarsdale Diet

DATE: / /

DAILY INTAKE

BREAKFAST

CALORIES

SNACK

CALORIES

LUNCH

CALORIES

SNACK

CALORIES

DINNER

CALORIES

WORKOUT

NOTES

Scarsdale Diet

DATE: / /

DAILY INTAKE

BREAKFAST

CALORIES

SNACK

CALORIES

LUNCH

CALORIES

SNACK

CALORIES

DINNER

CALORIES

WORKOUT

NOTES

Scarsdale Diet

DATE: / /

DAILY INTAKE

BREAKFAST

CALORIES

SNACK

CALORIES

LUNCH

CALORIES

SNACK

CALORIES

DINNER

CALORIES

WORKOUT

NOTES

Scarsdale Diet

DATE: / /

DAILY INTAKE

BREAKFAST

CALORIES

SNACK

CALORIES

LUNCH

CALORIES

SNACK

CALORIES

DINNER

CALORIES

WORKOUT

NOTES

Scarsdale Diet

DATE: / /

DAILY INTAKE

BREAKFAST

CALORIES

SNACK

CALORIES

LUNCH

CALORIES

SNACK

CALORIES

DINNER

CALORIES

WORKOUT

NOTES

Scarsdale Diet

DATE: ___ / ___ / ___

DAILY INTAKE

BREAKFAST

CALORIES

SNACK

CALORIES

LUNCH

CALORIES

SNACK

CALORIES

DINNER

CALORIES

WORKOUT

NOTES

Scarsdale Diet

DATE: / /

DAILY INTAKE

BREAKFAST

CALORIES

SNACK

CALORIES

LUNCH

CALORIES

SNACK

CALORIES

DINNER

CALORIES

WORKOUT

NOTES

Scarsdale Diet

DATE: / /

DAILY INTAKE

BREAKFAST

CALORIES

SNACK

CALORIES

LUNCH

CALORIES

SNACK

CALORIES

DINNER

CALORIES

WORKOUT

NOTES

Scarsdale Diet

DATE: / /

DAILY INTAKE

BREAKFAST

CALORIES

SNACK

CALORIES

LUNCH

CALORIES

SNACK

CALORIES

DINNER

CALORIES

WORKOUT

NOTES

Scarsdale Diet

DATE: / /

DAILY INTAKE

BREAKFAST

CALORIES

SNACK

CALORIES

LUNCH

CALORIES

SNACK

CALORIES

DINNER

CALORIES

WORKOUT

NOTES

Scarsdale Diet

DATE: / /

DAILY INTAKE

BREAKFAST

CALORIES

SNACK

CALORIES

LUNCH

CALORIES

SNACK

CALORIES

DINNER

CALORIES

WORKOUT

NOTES

Scarsdale Diet

DATE: / /

DAILY INTAKE

BREAKFAST

CALORIES

SNACK

CALORIES

LUNCH

CALORIES

SNACK

CALORIES

DINNER

CALORIES

WORKOUT

NOTES

Scarsdale Diet

DATE: / /

DAILY INTAKE

BREAKFAST

CALORIES

SNACK

CALORIES

LUNCH

CALORIES

SNACK

CALORIES

DINNER

CALORIES

WORKOUT

NOTES

Scarsdale Diet

DATE: / /

DAILY INTAKE

BREAKFAST

CALORIES

SNACK

CALORIES

LUNCH

CALORIES

SNACK

CALORIES

DINNER

CALORIES

WORKOUT

NOTES

Scarsdale Diet

DATE: / /

DAILY INTAKE

BREAKFAST

CALORIES

SNACK

CALORIES

LUNCH

CALORIES

WORKOUT

SNACK

CALORIES

NOTES

DINNER

CALORIES

Scarsdale Diet

DAILY INTAKE

BREAKFAST

CALORIES

SNACK

CALORIES

LUNCH

CALORIES

SNACK

CALORIES

DINNER

CALORIES

WORKOUT

NOTES

Scarsdale Diet

DATE: / /

DAILY INTAKE

BREAKFAST

	CALORIES

SNACK

	CALORIES

LUNCH

	CALORIES

SNACK

	CALORIES

DINNER

	CALORIES

WORKOUT

NOTES

Scarsdale Diet

DATE: / /

DAILY INTAKE

BREAKFAST

CALORIES

SNACK

CALORIES

LUNCH

CALORIES

SNACK

CALORIES

DINNER

CALORIES

WORKOUT

NOTES

Scarsdale Diet

DATE: / /

DAILY INTAKE

BREAKFAST

CALORIES

SNACK

CALORIES

LUNCH

CALORIES

SNACK

CALORIES

WORKOUT

NOTES

DINNER

CALORIES

Scarsdale Diet

DATE: ___ / ___ / ___

DAILY INTAKE

BREAKFAST

CALORIES

SNACK

CALORIES

LUNCH

CALORIES

SNACK

CALORIES

DINNER

CALORIES

WORKOUT

NOTES

Scarsdale Diet

DATE: / /

DAILY INTAKE

BREAKFAST

CALORIES

SNACK

CALORIES

LUNCH

CALORIES

SNACK

CALORIES

DINNER

CALORIES

WORKOUT

NOTES

Scarsdale Diet

DATE: / /

DAILY INTAKE

BREAKFAST

CALORIES

SNACK

CALORIES

LUNCH

CALORIES

SNACK

CALORIES

DINNER

CALORIES

WORKOUT

NOTES

Scarsdale Diet

DATE: / /

DAILY INTAKE

BREAKFAST

CALORIES

SNACK

CALORIES

LUNCH

CALORIES

SNACK

CALORIES

DINNER

CALORIES

WORKOUT

NOTES

Scarsdale Diet

DATE: / /

DAILY INTAKE

BREAKFAST

CALORIES

SNACK

CALORIES

LUNCH

CALORIES

SNACK

CALORIES

DINNER

CALORIES

WORKOUT

NOTES

Scarsdale Diet

DATE: ____ / ____ / ____

DAILY INTAKE

BREAKFAST

CALORIES

SNACK

CALORIES

LUNCH

CALORIES

SNACK

CALORIES

DINNER

CALORIES

WORKOUT

NOTES

Scarsdale Diet

DATE: / /

DAILY INTAKE

BREAKFAST

CALORIES

SNACK

CALORIES

LUNCH

CALORIES

SNACK

CALORIES

DINNER

CALORIES

WORKOUT

NOTES

Scarsdale Diet

DATE: / /

DAILY INTAKE

BREAKFAST

CALORIES

SNACK

CALORIES

LUNCH

CALORIES

SNACK

CALORIES

DINNER

CALORIES

WORKOUT

NOTES

Scarsdale Diet

DATE: / /

DAILY INTAKE

BREAKFAST

CALORIES

SNACK

CALORIES

LUNCH

CALORIES

SNACK

CALORIES

DINNER

CALORIES

WORKOUT

NOTES

Scarsdale Diet

DATE: / /

DAILY INTAKE

BREAKFAST	CALORIES

SNACK	CALORIES

LUNCH	CALORIES

SNACK	CALORIES

DINNER	CALORIES

WORKOUT

NOTES

Scarsdale Diet

DATE: / /

DAILY INTAKE

BREAKFAST

CALORIES

SNACK

CALORIES

LUNCH

CALORIES

SNACK

CALORIES

DINNER

CALORIES

WORKOUT

NOTES

Scarsdale Diet

DATE: /   /

DAILY INTAKE

BREAKFAST

CALORIES

SNACK

CALORIES

LUNCH

CALORIES

SNACK

CALORIES

DINNER

CALORIES

WORKOUT

NOTES

Scarsdale Diet

DATE: / /

DAILY INTAKE

BREAKFAST

CALORIES

SNACK

CALORIES

LUNCH

CALORIES

SNACK

CALORIES

DINNER

CALORIES

WORKOUT

NOTES

Scarsdale Diet

DAILY INTAKE

BREAKFAST

CALORIES

SNACK

CALORIES

LUNCH

CALORIES

SNACK

CALORIES

DINNER

CALORIES

WORKOUT

NOTES

Scarsdale Diet

DATE: / /

DAILY INTAKE

BREAKFAST

CALORIES

SNACK

CALORIES

LUNCH

CALORIES

SNACK

CALORIES

DINNER

CALORIES

WORKOUT

NOTES

Scarsdale Diet

DATE: / /

DAILY INTAKE

BREAKFAST

CALORIES

SNACK

CALORIES

LUNCH

CALORIES

SNACK

CALORIES

DINNER

CALORIES

WORKOUT

NOTES

Scarsdale Diet

DATE: / /

DAILY INTAKE

BREAKFAST

CALORIES

SNACK

CALORIES

LUNCH

CALORIES

SNACK

CALORIES

DINNER

CALORIES

WORKOUT

NOTES

Scarsdale Diet

DATE: / /

DAILY INTAKE

BREAKFAST		CALORIES

SNACK		CALORIES

LUNCH		CALORIES

SNACK		CALORIES

DINNER		CALORIES

WORKOUT

NOTES

Scarsdale Diet

DATE: / /

DAILY INTAKE

BREAKFAST	CALORIES

SNACK	CALORIES

LUNCH	CALORIES

SNACK	CALORIES

DINNER	CALORIES

WORKOUT

NOTES

Scarsdale Diet

DATE: /   /

DAILY INTAKE

BREAKFAST

CALORIES

SNACK

CALORIES

LUNCH

CALORIES

SNACK

CALORIES

DINNER

CALORIES

WORKOUT

NOTES

Scarsdale Diet

DATE: / /

DAILY INTAKE

BREAKFAST		CALORIES

SNACK		CALORIES

LUNCH		CALORIES

SNACK		CALORIES

DINNER		CALORIES

WORKOUT

NOTES

Scarsdale Diet

DATE: / /

DAILY INTAKE

BREAKFAST

CALORIES

SNACK

CALORIES

LUNCH

CALORIES

SNACK

CALORIES

DINNER

CALORIES

WORKOUT

NOTES

Scarsdale Diet

DATE: / /

DAILY INTAKE

BREAKFAST

CALORIES

SNACK

CALORIES

LUNCH

CALORIES

SNACK

CALORIES

DINNER

CALORIES

WORKOUT

NOTES

Scarsdale Diet

DATE: / /

DAILY INTAKE

BREAKFAST	CALORIES

SNACK	CALORIES

LUNCH	CALORIES

SNACK	CALORIES

DINNER	CALORIES

WORKOUT

NOTES

Scarsdale Diet

DATE: / /

DAILY INTAKE

BREAKFAST

CALORIES

SNACK

CALORIES

LUNCH

CALORIES

SNACK

CALORIES

DINNER

CALORIES

WORKOUT

NOTES

Scarsdale Diet

DATE: / /

DAILY INTAKE

BREAKFAST

CALORIES

SNACK

CALORIES

LUNCH

CALORIES

SNACK

CALORIES

DINNER

CALORIES

WORKOUT

NOTES

Scarsdale Diet

DATE: /   /

DAILY INTAKE

BREAKFAST

CALORIES

SNACK

CALORIES

LUNCH

CALORIES

SNACK

CALORIES

DINNER

CALORIES

WORKOUT

NOTES

Scarsdale Diet

DATE: / /

DAILY INTAKE

BREAKFAST

CALORIES

SNACK

CALORIES

LUNCH

CALORIES

SNACK

CALORIES

DINNER

CALORIES

WORKOUT

NOTES

Scarsdale Diet

DATE: / /

DAILY INTAKE

BREAKFAST

CALORIES

SNACK

CALORIES

LUNCH

CALORIES

SNACK

CALORIES

DINNER

CALORIES

WORKOUT

NOTES

Scarsdale Diet

DATE: / /

DAILY INTAKE

BREAKFAST

CALORIES

SNACK

CALORIES

LUNCH

CALORIES

SNACK

CALORIES

DINNER

CALORIES

WORKOUT

NOTES

Scarsdale Diet

DATE: / /

DAILY INTAKE

BREAKFAST

CALORIES

SNACK

CALORIES

LUNCH

CALORIES

SNACK

CALORIES

DINNER

CALORIES

WORKOUT

NOTES

Scarsdale Diet

DATE: ___ / ___ / ___

DAILY INTAKE

BREAKFAST | CALORIES

SNACK | CALORIES

LUNCH | CALORIES

SNACK | CALORIES

DINNER | CALORIES

WORKOUT

NOTES

Scarsdale Diet

DATE: ___/___/___

DAILY INTAKE

BREAKFAST

CALORIES

SNACK

CALORIES

LUNCH

CALORIES

SNACK

CALORIES

DINNER

CALORIES

WORKOUT

NOTES

Scarsdale Diet

DATE: / /

DAILY INTAKE

BREAKFAST

CALORIES

SNACK

CALORIES

LUNCH

CALORIES

SNACK

CALORIES

DINNER

CALORIES

WORKOUT

NOTES

Scarsdale Diet

DATE: ___ / ___ / ___

DAILY INTAKE

BREAKFAST

CALORIES

SNACK

CALORIES

LUNCH

CALORIES

SNACK

CALORIES

DINNER

CALORIES

WORKOUT

NOTES

Scarsdale Diet

DATE: / /

DAILY INTAKE

BREAKFAST

CALORIES

SNACK

CALORIES

LUNCH

CALORIES

WORKOUT

SNACK

CALORIES

NOTES

DINNER

CALORIES

Scarsdale Diet

DATE: / /

DAILY INTAKE

BREAKFAST

CALORIES

SNACK

CALORIES

LUNCH

CALORIES

SNACK

CALORIES

DINNER

CALORIES

WORKOUT

NOTES

Scarsdale Diet

DATE: / /

DAILY INTAKE

BREAKFAST

	CALORIES

SNACK

	CALORIES

LUNCH

	CALORIES

SNACK

	CALORIES

DINNER

	CALORIES

WORKOUT

NOTES

Scarsdale Diet

DATE: ___ / ___ / ___

DAILY INTAKE

BREAKFAST

CALORIES

SNACK

CALORIES

LUNCH

CALORIES

SNACK

CALORIES

DINNER

CALORIES

WORKOUT

NOTES

Scarsdale Diet

DATE: / /

DAILY INTAKE

BREAKFAST
CALORIES

SNACK
CALORIES

LUNCH
CALORIES

SNACK
CALORIES

DINNER
CALORIES

WORKOUT

NOTES

Scarsdale Diet

DATE: ___ / ___ / ___

DAILY INTAKE

BREAKFAST

CALORIES

SNACK

CALORIES

LUNCH

CALORIES

SNACK

CALORIES

DINNER

CALORIES

WORKOUT

NOTES

Scarsdale Diet

DATE: ___ / ___ / ___

DAILY INTAKE

BREAKFAST

CALORIES

SNACK

CALORIES

LUNCH

CALORIES

SNACK

CALORIES

DINNER

CALORIES

WORKOUT

NOTES

Scarsdale Diet

DATE: / /

DAILY INTAKE

BREAKFAST

CALORIES

SNACK

CALORIES

LUNCH

CALORIES

SNACK

CALORIES

DINNER

CALORIES

WORKOUT

NOTES

Scarsdale Diet

DATE: / /

DAILY INTAKE

BREAKFAST — CALORIES

SNACK — CALORIES

LUNCH — CALORIES

SNACK — CALORIES

DINNER — CALORIES

WORKOUT

NOTES

Scarsdale Diet

DATE: / /

DAILY INTAKE

BREAKFAST

CALORIES

SNACK

CALORIES

LUNCH

CALORIES

SNACK

CALORIES

DINNER

CALORIES

WORKOUT

NOTES

Scarsdale Diet

DATE: /   /

DAILY INTAKE

BREAKFAST

CALORIES

SNACK

CALORIES

LUNCH

CALORIES

SNACK

CALORIES

DINNER

CALORIES

WORKOUT

NOTES

Scarsdale Diet

DATE: / /

DAILY INTAKE

BREAKFAST

CALORIES

SNACK

CALORIES

LUNCH

CALORIES

SNACK

CALORIES

DINNER

CALORIES

WORKOUT

NOTES

Scarsdale Diet

DATE: / /

DAILY INTAKE

BREAKFAST

CALORIES

SNACK

CALORIES

LUNCH

CALORIES

SNACK

CALORIES

DINNER

CALORIES

WORKOUT

NOTES

Scarsdale Diet

DATE: / /

DAILY INTAKE

BREAKFAST

CALORIES

SNACK

CALORIES

LUNCH

CALORIES

SNACK

CALORIES

DINNER

CALORIES

WORKOUT

NOTES

Scarsdale Diet

DATE: /   /

DAILY INTAKE

BREAKFAST		CALORIES

SNACK		CALORIES

LUNCH		CALORIES

SNACK		CALORIES

DINNER		CALORIES

WORKOUT

NOTES

Scarsdale Diet

DAILY INTAKE

BREAKFAST

CALORIES

SNACK

CALORIES

LUNCH

CALORIES

SNACK

CALORIES

DINNER

CALORIES

WORKOUT

NOTES

Scarsdale Diet

DATE: /   /

DAILY INTAKE

BREAKFAST

CALORIES

SNACK

CALORIES

LUNCH

CALORIES

SNACK

CALORIES

DINNER

CALORIES

WORKOUT

NOTES

Scarsdale Diet

DATE: / /

DAILY INTAKE

BREAKFAST

CALORIES

SNACK

CALORIES

LUNCH

CALORIES

SNACK

CALORIES

DINNER

CALORIES

WORKOUT

NOTES

Check Out Our Other Journals

Planners

Daily Planners
Monthly Planners
Motivational Quote Planner
Our Wedding Planner
Project Planner

Diet Journals

17 Day Diet Journal
2 Day Diet Journal
8 Hours Diet Journal
Alkaline Diet Journal
Beyond Diet Journal
Biggest Loser Diet Journal
Blood Type Diet Journal
Candida Diet Journal
Caveman Diet Journal
Cleansing Diet Journal
Dash Diet Journal
Detox Diet Journal
Dukan Diet Journal
Eat To Live Diet Journal
Fast Metabolism Diet Journal
Fasting Diet Journal
Flat Belly Diet Journal
Fodmap Diet Journal
Juicing Diet Journal
Leptin Diet Journal
My Diet Journal
Paleo Diet Journal
Primal Diet Journal
Shred Diet Journal
Slow Carb Diet Journal
Wheat Belly Diet Journal

Cookbook & Recipes

Barbecue Recipes Journal
Cocktail Recipes Journal
Diabetes Recipes Journal
Eat To Live Recipes Journal
Juicing Recipes Journal
Kids Recipes Journal
Low Carb Recipes Journal
Mediterranean Recipes Journal
Paleo Recipes Journal
Pressure Cooker Recipes Journal
Slow Cooker Recipes Journal
Smoothies Recipes Journal
Vegan Recipes Journal

Journals

Action Journal
Anniversary Journal
Antique Journal
Bible Journal
Celtic Journal
Christian Journal
Crossfit Journal
Dream Journal
Expenses Journal
Fashion Journal
Five Minute Journal
Gardening Journal
Girl's Diary
Health Journal
Horse Journal
Inventor Journal
It's Gonna Be Okay Journal
Jesus Journal
Just Between Us Mother & Daughter
Kindergarten Journal
My Baby First 2 Years Journal
My Cruise Travel Diary
My Diaper Diary
My Dreambook
My Favorite Chocolate Journal
My Favorote Film Journal

Journals

My Favorite Music Journal
My Favorite Quotes Journal
My Gratitude Journal
My Home Projects Journal
My Ideas Journal
My Memories - Our Family Journal
My Photo Diary
My Quick One-Sentence A Day
Journal
My Restaurant Journal
My Wedding Diary
My Wellness Journal
Nature Journal
One LIne A Day Journal
Pet Journal
Prayer Journal
Pregnancy Journal
Q & A A Day Journal 5 Year
Q & A Journal
Question A Day
Strength Training
Teens Journal
The Minimalist Journal
Time Capsule Journal
Travel Journal
Wine Journal
Workout Journal
Yoga Journal

Other Journals

Address Book
Art Journal
Bucket List Journal
Drawing Book
Sketch Book
Password Journal

Journals available in
different languages:
English
French
German
Spanish

Made in the USA
Lexington, KY
21 April 2017